MOTHER
WATER
ASH

MOTHER WATER ASH

poems

NICOLE COOLEY

LOUISIANA STATE UNIVERSITY PRESS

BATON ROUGE

Published by Louisiana State University Press
lsupress.org

LSU Press Paperback Original

Designer: Michelle A. Neustrom
Typefaces: Whitman, text; Chong Modern, display

Cover illustration: *Breathing,* 2021, by Sibylle Peretti

Library of Congress Cataloging-in-Publication Data
Names: Cooley, Nicole, author.
Title: Mother water ash : poems / Nicole Cooley.
Other titles: Mother water ash (Compilation)
Description: Baton Rouge : Louisiana State University Press, 2024.
Identifiers: LCCN 2024009652 (print) | LCCN 2024009653 (ebook) |
    ISBN 978-0-8071-8246-8 (paperback) | ISBN 978-0-8071-8263-5 (epub) |
    ISBN 978-0-8071-8264-2 (pdf)
Subjects: LCGFT: Poetry.
Classification: LCC PS3553.O5647 M68 2024 (print) | LCC PS3553.O5647
    (ebook) | DDC 811/.54—dc23/eng/20240301
LC record available at https://lccn.loc.gov/2024009652
LC ebook record available at https://lccn.loc.gov/2024009653

in memory of my mother Jacqueline

and for my sister Alissa

Everything's moving, falling, slipping, vanishing . . .

—VIRGINIA WOOLF, "The Mark on the Wall"

CONTENTS

MOTHER
WATER
ASH

On the Mississippi River Levee, Styrofoam Cup in My Hand

that will disintegrate in 500 years   I drink my coffee   stand in gravel

     in my church skirt   black velvet I wore to my mother's funeral

eleven days ago   take a photo

   of my own shadow on the railroad tracks to Snapchat

to my daughters   while this river outside

my parents' house is rising higher than in years

       spillways opened   live oaks sunk in mud   grass

littered with plastic bags and beer cans   *Levee Trash: A Photo Essay*

my former self might think   that self so well-versed in irony

         that careful daughter   who would take notes

then shut her notebook   now on the levee

      a white truck speeds by too fast

maybe a man who picks up shifts on rigs for extra money

      and in a former life I'd write a poem

about how that man might be dangerous

      to my daughters   now I write

   nothing

I am here to walk off my restless

                                             sadness   to walk off my mother's voice

years ago after the storm when the city flooded   telling me she will never

leave New Orleans   no matter

how high water rises or how many times levees breach   telling me

                     she will die in her house

                     no evacuations   no hospitals

Now I know grief has its own topography   mine is

                         this city and this coast

～～～

Sixteen Years to the Day
Another Hurricane Reverses

the Mississippi's course   my father waits in our house

beside the river   and I dream my mother   drowning
water closing over her head   in my dreams she is always

dying   in the too-warm Gulf   then pricked alive again
fairy-tale spindle   my friends and I text each other

to describe dreams   in which our mothers
ask us why they're dead   New Orleans is the place

around which I uselessly orbit   after Katrina typing
my mother's name   *Missing Person Jacki Cooley*

into search engines   sixteen years ago my daughters asked
what is a hurricane's eye   what can it see

then my mother was alive   refusing to leave the city
now I text my father   *how high is the water   are there tornadoes*

phone and electric out   I wish for a slick of river
to spare our house   while in a new dream about my mother

she thrashes to the Gulf's sand floor   where she can't
burn or come apart

Missing

At the coffee shop before I pick up
    my daughters from school
        my mother three weeks dead

my tea tastes like smoke
    and I list all the seasons
        she is now missing

summer hot as the inside of a mouth
    winter when my hair freezes
        on my walk to the train

fall afternoon air rinsed cold
    trees ringed with dead leaves
        and I wear her coat

Grief is a river or it's an animal
    sharp-toothed and urgent
        When my first daughter was a baby

my mother said—of all I strived to do
    that my girl would not remember—
        She would know the absence of it—

My mother held my babies on her lap
    my mother taught me how
        to be a mother

Grief is a metronome clicking on my mother's piano
    while she watched
        me practice badly

Grief is the fact that my hands belong to her
    like hers my veins run too
        close to the skin

Grief is the fact that her hair
which never greyed
resembles mine

The absence of it

~~~~

With each Mississippi River flood, water spills out of the river.

Spill: a word too lovely.

Spill of grief, I write, cross out.

I'm taking too many notes.

A *floodlight's* fake illumination reveals nothing—

I want something tiny and unfindable—
my mother's ring, her thimble.

My desk is *flooded* with papers.

*Flood chat: to send a huge amount of data to another user.
Considered especially rude if the text is uninteresting.*

The television *floods* our dark bedroom with too many images.
Another storm. Another rising river. Fire.

Is this why my younger daughter cries or is she crying
for my mother?

Flood of tears. I only cry for my mother when
my daughters are at school,

when I sit at my desk to write everything down—

without my mother, without my girls who don't yet know
how much they miss—

My Mother's Ashtray

with the last of her DNA   gold clamshell I snap shut
now shoved under my couch to avoid   also to save

while I want my mother to return to offer me a list
of how I failed to snip a strand of her hair

at the funeral home for safe keeping   how
I never wore the skirts she sewed after my first love left

how when she visited to help with my babies   I refused
to let her smoke in the house   demanded she sit on the cold

porch with the ashtray   without her now I am back at the dark corner
of myself   the old urge to step out of my body   drop it

on the floor like a crumpled dress   skip a meal   run harder
as I lie on the floor of my daughter's room   fevered and finally

asleep   too old for this   in the middle of the night   I will
my mother to come back   to slip the ashtray out

from underneath the couch   ashtray I won't empty
should I save the butts her lips once touched   their own

museum exhibit   she won't return which means I fail
my mother   we called the skirts *the guilt skirts*

they still drape   folded stiff on a hanger   beside my girls' dresses
and her nightgowns my father gave me   I know she kept

the ashtray secret from my daughters   under the couch
ashed and ready   just as I collect my teenage daughters' baby clothes

in a box   ruffled toddler dress   blue sleep sack   just as
I wear her black raincoat now   as if my body could ever

be equivalent to hers   I flip the ashtray open like a beer can
or a jewelry box   a bed warmer to be held against a hearth fire

I research ashtrays on eBay to avoid myself   to not finish this poem
in which my mother is finally dead   and I have the evidence

in my house   this stick handle like a wrist

Monochords

1.

Grief: necklace burdening the throat, heft of a baby, bare legs gripping my hips.

2.

My mother held my babies best, nuzzled chin to chest, taught me how to give a first bath to my first daughter in a plastic tub on the kitchen table.

3.

Grief: a crape myrtle tree branch snags against my wrist, and I am ten and I swallow a chip of my mother's black soap, a present from my father, from her nightgown drawer.

4.

Once breath pressed out of her body.

5.

I hate all the people who still have mothers.

6.

My mother slipped peaches into the mouth of my first girl in her highchair; taught my second daughter to read.

7.

She taught me breath against skin, proof a child is breathing, and I watch the rise and fall of my daughter against my mother's chest.

8.

Repeated dream after my mother dies where I find dragonflies the size of palms and wonder if they came from my body or hers—

9.

Care: *a burdened state of mind, as that arising from heavy responsibilities; worry.*

10.

How my mother *took care.* How my mother took care of my daughters. How my mother—

11.

How we did not know she was dying.

12.

Care: *charge, custody, keeping, supervision; trust in watching, guarding, overseeing.*

13.

How I never sat by her bed all night while she slept nor wondered whether I would be able—

14.

Objects that will now forever make me sad:

15.

Care: *mental suffering; grief. An object or source of worry, attention, or solicitude.*

16.
Objects: Salem 100s. Velvet dollhouse curtains. Mixing bowl. Her handwriting.

17.
She who *took care*—

18.
No fentanyl patch, fly-paper sticky, no pills to grind under my heel as I slam out the door.

19.
No *taking care*, hand on a back, over a shoulder, no surgical glove,

                                     shiver of silver and green—

Still Life, South Galvez Street, 1978

"Stay upstairs," my mother tells me. "Take care of your sister." Inside our house, floodwaters are rising

Inch-by-inch, foot-by-foot, our basement brims with water. Rain lashes the windows. Parish drainage pumps have failed. My sister and I stand at the top of the basement stairs, watching my dollhouse, the house my mother built from scratch, painted, and decorated, the house for which she sewed four dolls, each the size of a finger, replicas of each member of our family.

Everything in the basement is ruined, and I am a selfish, bad daughter who cares only about her dollhouse.

For three days, we don't go to school. We don't leave the house. We sit at the top of the basement stairs. Floodwater does not drain. Water rises to my dollhouse's edge, swirls over the cobblestone path that circles the house. I wish for the interior of the house, all six rooms, painted a shiny, enameled pink, to stay dry and safe. Portraits she made from postcards and hung on the walls. Rugs she crocheted. Canopy bed she built.

In the basement, the water is now a foot deep. "The water is full of chemicals and run-off from the street," my mother says. "Stay right there." Toxic or not, the water rises, and she wades through it, barefoot.

The levees do not break, no floodwalls crack. Yet nothing in the basement can be saved. Except my dollhouse.

Proof of my mother's magic: she built me my own house that can't ever be destroyed.

~~~~

Twenty miles from the Gulf of Mexico's coast,
I wrote in my notebook, at the edge of St. Mary Parish.
Low coastal marshes, ridges of alluvial land.

And we are losing it.

Rigs stretched over the Gulf like flightless birds
over sand and billboards, all steadily erasing.

Seventy miles west of New Orleans is Morgan City,
the gateway to the Gulf!

It was high school and the lesson was about the Nearly Gone
but we were sixteen and bored.

Film voice-over too loud and bright, rows of desks
too close, classroom too dark—

In 1947, the first offshore oil well was drilled, very far
from any land or citizens, perfectly safe, beginning a new era
for the state, a black gold rush.

I copied facts and watched the rain out the science classroom window,
sewers and gutters filling, brimming, afternoon storm water
as usual with nowhere to go.

Mother Water Ash

Mother gone to ash   river gone to drowned
I don't live here anymore   as my friends remind

Now I walk the edge of the Grand Central Parkway
Flushing Meadows Park   world's fair gone dark

what is ashed and drowned   what is abandoned
Mother gone   drowned in her body the night

she died alone in New Orleans   ashed her cigarette
then left us   did I go dark when the N train lost power

on my way home   while the burning threaded through
my baby's hair   city doused in ash   impossible

to keep the outside out   River Road beside my parents' house
leads to *Cancer Alley*   Mother gone   but once with her

I drove through the drowned city   two months after
the storm   yellowed grass   houses gone   the road

a slur of empty   is it any wonder I've followed her advice
to subtract myself   good daughter always   till I'm not

did I go dark when she left me   when will my daughters
while my mother's mouth is all slick black feathers

Breathwork

Now I say *mom* and I float to the ceiling.

~~~~~

Breath: *meaning "ability to breathe," hence "life," is from ca. 1300. Meaning "a single act of breathing," from the late fifteenth century; sense of "the duration of a breath, a moment, a short time," from the early thirteenth century. Meaning "a breeze, a movement of free air."*

~~~~~

Five months ago in New Orleans my mother stopped breathing.

Now at yoga class in the final posture, *Savasana,* pose I struggle with most because I must sink into stillness, and I know it's wrong but I imagine a lit cigarette between my fingers.

My mother taught me well and carefully, and with gifts. In high school, she bought me cigarettes so I would not eat.

~~~~~

Breath: *from an Old English word for "odor, scent, stink, exhalation, vapor." Old English for "air exhaled from the lungs."*

~~~~~

Now I mourn my mother through breath.

~~~~~

Each morning, I stretch out on a mat in a hot room and squeeze my eyes shut and breathe her in. Or breathe her out. Yes, breath should anchor me, but I use it to exit my body, just as my mother taught me. I rise to the ceiling of the yoga room, alone and untethered.

I wish to lie on the levee in the dirt and gravel.

Instead I lie on the mat miles away from the house where she died.

~~~~

Drown   smoke   suffocate   What is the difference?

~~~~

I close my eyes and in my dream my mother drowns in the river two blocks from her house.

In another dream I shake her awake. I ask her, with frustration, if she will go on being dead.

~~~~

I only practice hot yoga, want infrared heat that spills from vents and warms the floor. I love the punishing. And the intense heat echoes a New Orleans levee walk, all stifling humidity. I lower my body into plank, crush my breasts to the ground. Think of my mother's body.

~~~~

Breath: *from Proto-Germanic* bræthaz *for "smell, exhalation."*

~~~~

As a teenager, I'd come home from school to find a carton of Benson & Hedges on my white bedspread. My mother Saran-wrapped and labeled all my food with calorie counts. *25. 50. 75.*

Inside the refrigerator's wedge of light, I counted.

Unwrapped a pack of cigarettes. *It will keep you from being hungry,* my mother explained.

Celery. Grapefruit. Diet bread thin as dress fabric.

A lighter she pressed into my hands.

~~~~

Breath: *an act of breathing: fought to the last breath.*

~~~~

Yoga reminds me of the geometry of the body, the shape the body makes.

What shape did my mother's body make on the living-room floor? What shape was her mouth when my father pressed his mouth to hers to perform useless CPR?

What shape was she under the sheet on the stretcher at the Veterans Boulevard funeral home—who knew funeral homes have stretchers and if you don't pay for a coffin you get that?—when she looked so small and thin, and what shape was she—altered?—when my sister and my father and I ran back to her to kiss her for a final time?

~~~~

Drown   suffocate   smoke

~~~~

The irony is that after my mother dies, we eat. My father, my sister, and me. Friends bring platters and trays and Tupperware.

The kind of meals I would not normally allow myself. The kind of food my mother forbade.

Red beans and rice with sausage. Baked ziti. Cheesecake. Doughnuts. A half-bottle of wine.

~~~~

Now at yoga class I fill my lungs with imaginary smoke. I imagine I flick a cigarette lighter over and over, on and off, till my thumb scrapes with ache.

~~~~

Breath: *opportunity or time to breathe; respite. Also, a slight breeze.*

~~~~

I'm lying on the mat. Under the heat vent. Or I am just under—as grief's water closes over my head.

~~~~

My teenage daughters think the stories about my mother telling me to smoke are very strange. *This was the eighties—a different time,* I explain.

~~~~

Three days after she is dead, my sister and I clean out our mother's closet and find seventy-two cartons of Salem 100s hidden in boxes labeled "Taxes 2003" and "Family Medical 2010."

Over and over, my mother often told me when we were alone, "I'll never stop smoking." Defiant.

Then why did she hide them like contraband?

Breath—

~~~~~

Mother's Day yoga is, as I knew it would be, the worst. Why did I go? The teacher suggests we dedicate our practice to "your mother or a mother figure in your life" and I feel tears leaking out the sides of my eyes. Later she returns to it: "Think of the mother or mother figure and focus on a happy memory."

I want to ban this language. I want to run from the room.

Instead I just work as hard as I can to not imagine it: the crematorium, my mother's body on a shelf, flames, body who once housed my body, turning to nothing.

~~~~~

For so long I wished for another body—is this my mother's fault?

What could I tell you about my relationship to my body and my mother?

What could she say now?

~~~~~

A different time, I tell my daughters.

~~~~~

Missing my mother is a pain that feels bone deep.

My wrists splinter. My hips lock shut. My jawbone burns.

~~~~~

After my mother dies, all I want, predictably, is to smoke. Though I have not had a cigarette in more than twenty years.

I suck on one of her old cigarette butts in the ashtray, set my lips where hers imprinted, while my sister watches, alarmed.

Putting my mouth where her mouth once was.

~~~~

Do you want to go in and say goodbye to her feel free to take all the time you need to say goodbye to her—

~~~~

What would my mother tell me now?

What will I tell my daughters?

~~~~

Once, in my twenties, I remember my mother taking a photograph of me after a bad breakup when I stopped eating, a photo at the edge of a pool while I posed in a blue striped bikini.

I knew at that moment that for the first time my mother was proud of my body.

As my sister and I finish cleaning out our mother's closet, I recall this photo, and we toss the cigarette cartons in the trash.

~~~~

Breath: *a spoken sound: utterance. Also, spirit, animation.*

Missing

Grief is rage and it is a visible thing, I text to myself. Not a brick hurled at a face or a fist in a throat but this: my mother's red striped shirt that she will never wear again, lying on the floor. Or later at the columbarium, the low drag of the screws shutting up a marble slab. Just ashes in a box. My mother hidden, sealed, gone. *I am too full of rage,* I text to myself, on the plane down to New Orleans after she is dead, and beside me is a grandma. Holding a fussy baby. And when I try to connect with her, as I do with anyone holding a baby on a plane, she looks at me blankly: "It's just separation anxiety." That first night in New Orleans texted to myself while I lie on the couch, wearing her nightgown: *Everywhere I am is a place I don't want to be.*

~~~~~

Another summer of the vanishing. Summer
after my mother's death.

Summer of the country turning from more loss.
Everyone is *tired* of fires and floods:
Cities stacked like a deck, spread on a table, shuffled,
reshuffled. Field overrun with
water. Another city burning.

Summer of flames from one coast to another,
summer of skies ashed to darkness.

Drown   Suffocate   Smoke:
so many ways to wreck the world while we watch.

An easy rhythm, what Freud called *Fort-Da*.
Loss and Recovery.
I recall my toddler daughter dropping a cracker

for my mother to retrieve then return,
to ensure the Not Gone and the Never Gone,
to prove the world still standing,
object permanence.

My mother and I watching. Our job
to always show my girl
things don't disappear.

Still Life, Jefferson Highway

For three weeks after our mother dies, my sister and I return to New Orleans and live outside of time and space—no jobs, no husbands, no children—and I am now sleeping on the couch where she died, wearing her nightgown, which I have washed and washed and yet still smells like smoke.

Each night my father spills out two blue sleeping pills into my palm.

~~~~~

unmothered motherless motherfree not a mother no mother

~~~~~

Each morning, for three weeks in New Orleans I walk Jefferson Highway.

Prestige Flooring, Ochsner Hospital, Dat Bar, Zaddie's Tavern, kudzu-covered lot where the Sports Palace was, Section 8 housing, dumpster behind the dry cleaners.

There is beauty elsewhere in this city, but I choose to ignore it.
Forget magnolia and hibiscus.

I walk past the hospital where she did not go to die.

~~~~~

One of the biggest surprises: grief resides deep in the body. I'm shaky and dizzy and can't balance and shivering and I am in New Orleans and it is not cold.

Now I hate spring, the greening of the trees, the budding; the peonies forcing themselves out of the dirt in the yard make me furious.

~~~~~

Once her body was my home.

~~~~

Another surprise: at times my father, sister, and I are hungry. We spoon up all the red beans and rice friends brought. Eat too much cake.

Mornings in New Orleans are the worst: I am awake and blasted by church hymns, which screech through my head then make me dizzy.

~~~~

What was she wearing when they burned her body?

~~~~

I remember how she faked her death when I was a child: in our family play, *Hansel and Gretel.*

She was the bad stepmother, a kitchen knife slipped between
her arm and her shoulder and she fell down on the floor.

~~~~

When I wake up: "Hail Thee, Festival Day" on an organ. She knew how to play.

~~~~

Spring: season of renewal, season that doesn't exist in New Orleans, no cool wind rinsing the air, none of the bulbs we never planted that always come back rising from the earth in front of the house.

~~~~

Texted to myself while I walk the highway: *You must remember her reading aloud.*

She always did the voices. She was a much better reader than my father, which still surprises. I hear her voice in my head so easily whenever I read now.

I wish I had read to my daughters in that way, wish I took the pleasure in it that she did. I wanted to read my own book and sit beside them.

Now I can't read. This oddly comforts.

~~~~

I put on her winter hat, worn only when she visited us on the East Coast.

At night I stretch out on the couch, shaking under sheets as if under the surface of water, under the Gulf, the water she said she sat by to question God, to mourn the loss of our sister, her stillborn third child, the loss that almost took her faith, she said.

~~~~

The priest insists on an afterworld. I want to believe it.

~~~~

I was the last to touch her.

Not her body but the box of her ashes.

In the columbarium I touched the white cloth—shroud?—covering the wooden box that was her. I rested my hand on the cloth, on the top of the box, told her I loved her—

~~~~

At her funeral, the man who followed me around the city for years when I was a teenager, taking photos of my body, approached me, stuck his finger in his eye, and dragged it wetly down my face. "I cried for your mother. I want you to know," he said. Why was he at her funeral?

I should have been shocked but I wasn't.

~~~~

Before I walk onto the highway, I snap the head off a pansy in the front yard. I want to ruin something.

~~~~

Why do I have hives the night before her funeral? I feel heat rising in the skin of my face and stare at it for differences—aren't I a completely different person now, and why can no one see it?

Something is burning beneath my surface.

~~~~

I am walking the highway. I am smoking her cigarette.

~~~~

My sister and I throw out all the cigarettes in black contractor bags behind the house. But her lighters are a problem. Research on my phone reveals a single lighter can ignite a landfill, and my sister and I agree we have to take action—we carry them all to Zaddie's Tavern on the corner of the highway across from our parents' house.

The bar is hot and thick with smoke, empty except for a man hunched over a machine playing video poker.

"Could you use any of these?" I ask the woman behind the bar.

"Oh yes, and thanks," she says, with a broad smile, looking happier than the nurse at the hospital where my sister and I donated our mother's glasses the day before. "Oh, yes, we can."

My Mother's Nightgowns Smell Like Smoke

White cotton, with buttons the size of baby teeth.

Each morning, in one of her nightgowns and my black winter boots, I drive my daughters to school, and as they climb out of the car, I want to crawl out of my own skin, everything prickly and hesitant.

~~~~

I'm on the elliptical trainer at the YMCA beside my younger daughter who wears a black *Thrasher* T-shirt. She doesn't skateboard, doesn't live in California. And a few days later, on my way to fly to my father after my mother dies, I see many teen girls in the airports I pass through wearing that exact shirt. *Skateboarding is a dangerous sport. You could break bones,* I caution my daughters that night from New Orleans, on the phone as I sit on my parents' bed, in the house without my mother, as if now I could protect anyone's fragile body.

~~~~

We called them *the guilt skirts,* the three skirts she sewed for me when I broke up with my graduate school boyfriend and she knew she didn't help me when I cried. She mailed me the skirts instead. One with flowers, one green, one gray. I never wore them. Now the skirts hang bunched in my closet beside my daughter's abandoned prom dress.

~~~~

In New Orleans, my mother has been dead for three days, and I wake up and my hands are shaking and my sister and I drive to the Salvation Army Family Store on Jefferson Highway and drop off another trash bag of her clothes. *It's my happy place,* I tell my sister, and I am being ironic and *using humor as a coping mechanism* as at least one grief podcast recommends, but it's also true, and she agrees, as we finger racks of dresses. We can't leave till I find something that is a channel back to her. In the dressing room, I sweat through velvet in someone else's too-tight blouse.

~~~~

The fake-French café where I have disappeared to write about my mother in Brooklyn is advertising "Bastille Day specials" and I remember Bastille Day in New Orleans in 1976, and how my mother sewed my sister and me cancan dresses: satin and rainbow nylon net to kick up in ruffled layers. All summer, we wore the dresses every day and slept in them, in our twin beds, in our girl bodies, when we were still daughters.

Missing

My mother is a fish, Vardaman repeats, in Faulkner's *As I Lay Dying,* as his family builds his dying mother's coffin. My favorite novel in college. It comes back now. On the beach on my pink bike wearing my mother's bathing suit I ride as fast as I can past dead fish after dead fish, choked by the algae. Deprived of oxygen, they must have thrown their bodies gasping on the sand. Like my mother, I think, unable to breathe, dying, and then am aghast at my own terrible metaphor, which she would hate. If I waded out in the water, color of rust, color of blood, if I let the water close over my head, would that shrink the distance between us?

~~~~

Once the coastline spoke: *I plan to disappear and tell you nothing.*

Geographic body, etched on a map. Count the houses where families live,

where a river splinters, salt water surges

through a channel built for ships and oil, dredged and leveed,

children die. To myself, I spoke:

You need to be less daughter, *you need*

to go home to your own daughters,

to be a mother, to stop walking the Mississippi's edge. But the Gulf

is burning, marshes disappearing, sidewalk buckling

like a choking throat. The coastline advises:

Count my waves. Count the days your mother

has been gone. Count the hurricanes, the floods,

the times the water unspooled and didn't drown the town.

Monochords

1.
Shelter of Last Resort—the Superdome in August 2005 where I told you to go.

2.
Shelter, as if final—the columbarium behind the church where your ashes are interred. How I hate the word *interred* for its blankness, its lightness in the mouth.

3.
Shelter in place, the history teacher tells my daughter, as she and her classmates stack chairs against the door during another active-shooter drill.

4.
Shelter that is not the body you taught me to distrust but is the pink miniature house you built for me.

5.
Shelter that is not the ruined houses we saw two months post-Katrina driving the city, yards piled with trash, tables, chairs, a refrigerator stamped with a girl's school portraits.

6.
Shelter that is not an X scribbled on a house that means *a body found.*

Being the Oldest Daughter

My mother's death is another body: she flaunts herself, takes up too much
space in my bed, ruins my closet, wears my best black skirt,
side-zipped up her thigh. Spins and twirls in my slip,
color of a baby aspirin, color of a dulled sun.

As if now my mother refuses
to be a mother, has no interest in the children
who cry for her, demand sippy cups of milk, want
to settle in her arms in a favorite green chair.
She won't touch them, refuses every embrace.

But don't worry: soon her death will undress herself; she'll unveil,
but never in the dark, she wants all the lights on,
she loves cheap fluorescence.

Silence

Don't talk to me about the throat, the lungs, any red road to the body's interior.
Don't talk to me about how, for so long, it was my favorite metaphor.
Now I picture my mother's lungs.

Being the Oldest Daughter

who gets the texts on her phone: *Peace, love, and strength to you!*
Thinking of you! Stay strong!
Who is offered gifts of scented bath crystals, body wash.
Important to stay clean and lovely.

Let me know what you need, people say.
Maybe I need nothing.

Metaphors for a Different Ending

An endoscope's black fish tail.
PET scan machine a big plastic donut, unsugared.
MRI, loud as a car crash.
IV drip a watery popsicle.

But she refused all treatment.

And so the tenor and the vehicle split apart.

Being the Oldest Daughter

Walking out of the hospital into late morning
brightness in New Orleans with my sister,
after giving away all our mother's glasses,
on Jefferson Highway, watching the people our age,
perfectly healthy and well,
people who still have mothers,

I'm filled with fury at everyone's good health—

The Tenor and the Vehicle

Grief is a plate scraped clean.

Grief is a sun-bleached sheet. Or none.
Or neither.
It's a kitchen dishrag,
stuffed at the back of a drawer,
torn, mildew dark—

Mourning, Silk and Lace

Clouds scalloped white as the collar of a girl's Sunday dress—
banner below the sky: *Millsent Connor, Her Work Aged Ten, Boston, 1799.*

In her sampler, silk on linen, everything is paired. Woman stands
in a doorway. Woman walking on a path. Two men. Animals:

a horse and a dog. Double rows of pink potted flowers. Two houses
starred with branches. Two birds backstitched into the air. I picture the girl,

a daughter, bent over cloth in a kitchen chair, alone. The first small knot
will be a rose along the border. Her mother is seven days dead.

Lace filling stitch: now this girl threads red brick to build a house
she will never live in. There are no daughters in this new world. Also

no mothers. Only women dressed in white, waiting. Reversible stitch:
I can't understand the symmetry so I invent a story. All knots.

All tying-off of thread.   When I imagine a world—single
satin stitch—why do I always return to mother and daughter?

To the word *bereft?* To the daughter after a mother's death?
Silk on linen. I backstitch to this girl, to her past, to doubled

blooming plants, as she sits dizzy and untethered, studying
her work. In silence. What does it mean to be *bereaved*

and why do I imagine her so? *Bereft* meaning also: *deprived or robbed.*
Yet we are all of course untethered. Fishbone stitch. We all wait

for grief. We all walk out on a path to nothing. Meanwhile in the kitchen,
a girl wishes herself two. Silk and linen. Spill of dirt.

~~~~~

Could the California fires ever fill the Mississippi
with ash? Slow burn on another coast.
Could I snip my mother's hair, seal it in a locket, skip
the stone of it across the river, or
nestle a tangle in a sparrow's nest?
There is my mother's body and
then there is the "dead zone."
Meanwhile, the heat is a record this year.
Meanwhile, scientists predict:
the summer dead zone in the Gulf
will be the biggest in our history.
Meanwhile, the chemicals spilled into
the Atchafalaya, the Mississippi—
runoff from the Midwest floods—
could cover nearly 8,800 square miles.
Meanwhile, the dead zone is the size of New Jersey.

Missing

When it's too hot in my New Jersey house I split
open the old window inside our bedroom closet

constructed from the hallway and lie down,
curl up under my daughter's baby quilt on the closet

floor. Impossible to explain the solace and comfort
of lying alone inside my tiny closet,

beside my mother's clothes: her red sweater,
her boots, her long dresses I keep closest

to me but will never wear, her black raincoat
with the broken zipper I won't fix, her clothes

that won't fit me because she was so small. My body
outpaced hers. I keep living. I keep my daughters close

to honor her, yet I never did snip the hem off
her shirt to slide into a mourning locket. Yet I closed

my eyes when I first saw her body on the gurney
at the funeral home, her name not spelled out anywhere—

Still Life, River Road

On the morning of August 29, 2015, ten years into the After, I walk with my mother to the levee two blocks from our house.

Yes, she says. *They raised the levee because of Katrina, about three feet.*

We stand together and stare out at the Mississippi.

~~~~~

It is difficult not to believe we are living through a time of environmental catastrophe, I read, browsing the news outside of my own body on my phone as I walk back to my parents' house after my mother dies.

My parents' house—or, no longer my parents' house, now my fathers' house—set between Jefferson Highway and River Road.

~~~~~

Nothing in this city feels safe now. Or did it ever—

~~~~~

I hear my mother's voice.

~~~~~

Levee: *from the Medieval Latin for* "embankment." *Then* Levee *into English by way of French:* "to raise, to lighten."

~~~~~

All that tenth-anniversary weekend in New Orleans, as I walk the streets of the city, attend events, talk to people, I keep thinking about the language we used and still use to talk about Katrina. I think about *crevasse* and *levee,* about *storm* and *flood*, about (two terms we need to trouble) *"natural"* and *"human made"* disasters.

And I remember my first time back in New Orleans in the fall of 2005, how I cataloged the debris I saw from the car window. My mother and I drove around the city, all the streetlights out, front yards and curbs full of garbage that was really people's entire lives emptied from their ruined houses.

My lists useless yet I could not stop writing them.

A slab of wallboard.
A baby blanket.
A single drawer.
A ketchup bottle.

Door a blank eyehole.

~~~~~

In 2006, the first anniversary, I sat in the Convention Center at a prayer service for the city where a pastor pronounced Katrina a Cesarean section, a "birth gone wrong," but told us that now we "stand in the delivery room of opportunity."

And a few weeks later a piece in the *Chicago Tribune* stated, "Hurricane Katrina gave a great American city a rebirth."

And I came home and told my mother.

~~~~~

FEMA. The Road Home. The Unified New Orleans Plan. The Green Dot Map.

~~~~~

Now there is no one to tell.
My mother is not here.
Now the city goes on without her.

~~~~

As I walk home from church along the levee, I remember how my mother told me: *Katrina will never be used to name any North Atlantic hurricane again.*

On April 6, 2006, the World Meteorological Organization, at the request of the U.S. government, cited the horrific destructive power of Katrina as a reason to officially retire the name.

~~~~

Mourning. Observation. Celebration. Eulogy. Commemoration. To Commemorate: *to recall and show respect for (someone or something); to mark or celebrate (an event or person) by doing or producing something.*

~~~~

To raise, to lighten. Fifteen years now after the storm.

Missing

Two months after my mother dies, while listening to a grief podcast, I clean out the refrigerator at my father's house, thinking, *Why are so many of the words to depict grief so lovely?*

Keen. Wail. Weep. Bereavement. I've already overused these words. I've been wastefully drawn to them for years.

As if now I don't want to climb out of my own body, as if a pair of hands doesn't keep catching and catching in my hair.

On the Levee Once Again I Walk to Sharpen

my body to a blade   weapon for nothing   recall
my first diet   sixty-six pounds   proud refusal of a milk carton

or my mother's sister at forty   spooning Gerber peaches
into her mouth at the family table   or the game

my mother taught me at fourteen   *find someone*
on the street who has my body   how she taught me always

to compare   how without her still I've sworn   to be
vapor   still furious at the world   rushing through

the year's dark corridor   third year without her
street unspooling   before me   tracking my miles

how I once   how I still   desire   her judgment
be vapor   be smoke   be blade   remember how

it feels to desire   nothing   not even touch's static
why   emptiness still comforts   like nothing else

I shrink myself to   where I don't matter
Thumbelina   tight and safe in a walnut shell

yet grief thickens everything   even the imprint of my body

who's keeping count

~~~~

Ten years into the After, the Mississippi
is a Ouija board my mother
gave my daughters and the four of us watch
its swerve and sway,

beside a snowball truck,
as the girls spoon pink ice onto the grass
scrubbed yellow and dry,

the shoreline made fragile by empty spaces,
concrete foundations marked *No Trespassing*.

Now, if I could go back to this moment,
here's what I would want most:
to be in the middle of things
with my mother and my daughters—

Deluge. Drown. Engulf. Flush.
Inundate. Overflow.

After My Mother Dies I Crave the Seventies

First the foods. Deviled eggs scattered with paprika. A Bloody
Mary, celery stuck in the center of the glass. A cheese log

studded with cloves. Bowl of green goddess dressing. All of the decade's
weird nourishment, foods I never ate as a child. Yet now I ache stupidly

for the cold orb of that egg, its shirred and dusted yolk. And then I want
to go running in the New Orleans park with a Walkman, sweaty Styrofoam

slipping from my ears, rectangular weight in my hand. I want to dial
a rotary phone and call my mother back. And when I find her—

she and I will watch *Klute* and *Midnight Cowboy* together
on our green and yellow fiberglass couch. Crave:

from the Old English, meaning, "ask, implore, demand by right."
My mother and I are back at the Winn Dixie on the highway and she

is younger than I am now and I am asking for a mood ring
from the gumball machine. Crave: *perhaps related to "craft"*

in its base sense of "power." And now I want my mother to be
my sister which is ridiculous as I have a sister and I am raising two sisters

in my other life as a mother. Meanwhile I am back in our living room
in New Orleans and my mother and I are shoving

the particleboard bookcases against the wall and flipping open
our TAB cans. I want my cheap acrylic turtleneck back. I want

my IBM Selectric to type my middle school papers. My Betamax. My
8-track tapes. My early Billy Joel. After we rearrange the living room

in the hopes of changing our lives, my mother and I fold
a paper fortune teller together and I quiz her—*yes, no, maybe.*

She gives no good answers. But after all she is back from the dead.
In the other world, which is this one, my daughters have the box

of my parents' Ouija board and are scooting the planchette
over cardboard, late at night, while my husband and I sleep

upstairs. Crave: *to long for, eagerly desire; to ask very earnestly.*
Deviled eggs were first made in ancient Rome where it was said,

From eggs to apples, meaning from a beginning to its end,
in the course of a meal. Eggs the color of the couch my mother

and I sat on when I believed she would never die.

My Mother's Matches

A birdcage opens in my mother's chest to expose
her ruined lungs while
I open her shoebox, saved matchbooks
from Texas and Georgia.
Who knew she kept so many, I think, then:
Were they for when the hurricane hit, the power out?
I need to call my sister. Inside the birdcage
is pure, clean air. But my mother's body is all
darkness now—I am the oldest daughter of an oldest
daughter, inheriting her deep unease in a body.
How to connect is always the question—
here are the facts: packets of purple
K&B matches, New Orleans drugstore, shuttered
not long ago, matchbook flaps like birds' wings
I spread out on my desk. K&B, where E
and I stole Bonne Bell Lip Smackers and
were caught. My mother furious. *Katz and Bestoff*—
first store opened in 1905 on Canal by
a pharmacist and a drugstore owner from Memphis—
purple as my childhood house's front door.
My favorite color, also my sister's, my brother's, my father's.
What was my mother's favorite color? None of us know.
My mother known for smoking and for love.
While what about the ruin inside
myself, tiny burned-out fire, little pile
of kindling sticks? I want to believe if I swallow a match,
I will bring back my mother.
As if my mother's smoking was a form of love? Of course not.
Yet I go back to her matches—ever the good daughter who
she taught to name and label,
just as K&B's slogan was: *Take it personally.*
Matchbook all butterfly wings or a spatchcocked chicken.
When I strike a match, I recall
my mother rinsing my hair over the sink,
tip of silver pitcher against my neck,

heat's friction I thrilled to.
How is my mother not in the earth
but burned and set inside stone in the columbarium,
enough above the waterline to be saved from the next flood
in our city? How is it I wish against all wishes
I could still light her cigarette, offer it to her soured mouth?

Elegy, Napoleon House, New Orleans

And a year now past her death and I am "better"—I am not eating her foods,
not pouring ranch dressing on cottage cheese, both of which I hate,

and shoveling it in my mouth. And I am not starving myself to echo her body.
Also I am not lying on the floor, curled like a shrimp, only to rouse myself

when my girls get home from school to stop my crying. Yet grief does not
sharpen over time nor does it—as I once believed—loosen. It is just a weight.

My limbs feel so heavy. My shoulders burn. My wrists ache deeply. Next to me,
the two men at the table are talking about grief. "Grief is not something

you get through," one says. They are middle-aged. One just lost his father.
"The thing about immediate grief . . ." the man begins, but he doesn't finish.

The second quotes Saul Bellow—"Losing a parent is like driving through a plate-
glass window." Eavesdropping, I immediately Google and can't find it anywhere.

"Are you sleeping?" one asks, and I am thinking how after she died the carpet
in my mother's room was so full of smoke it spread like a stain. I am thinking

how my childhood is now over. I am thinking about how I wish grief would
sharpen the world. Instead it dulls and dulls and dulls.

Razor blade wiped too many times on a towel.

Monochords

1.
How to keep the water out of metaphor—*you will drown in me.*

2.
Once I floated in my mother's body.

3.
Count the floods on your fingers an abacus.

4.
I want the weight of gravel in my hand then flung on the levee.

5.
I want stones stinging my skin crushed oyster shells in a parking lot.

6.
I took my daughters to the river   I walked with my mother.

7.
My mother was the first person to teach me how to leave my body.

New Orleans Love Poem

As my tongue runs
down your spine in bed,
outside my parents' house
sea levels are rising,
the city filling, flooding,
predicted to disappear
in a hundred years. Outside
the sky is glazed with light,
soap white. The Mississippi
shimmers. So much beauty.
So how wrong is it
to stay in this room?
To hold each other,
to keep our bodies
safe and alone together?
This house—pink stucco
latticed with mold,
water bubbles in the streets
from storm drains. Asphalt cracks.
And on our screens
bad news unfurls—
War. Fire. Drought.
In my childhood room, you mouth me open.
I close my hands
over your shoulders
then remember driving
to pick up our daughters
while a story about "ecological grief"
played on NPR,
the summer after my mother died.
Outside: magnolia tree lashed with rain.
Tongue. Mouth. Hair.
How wrong is it now to take solace
in the ordinary?
We slide out of our clothes.

A hundred years from now
when the world churns on
without us, the bridge drowns,
braceleted with light.
And here we are, in another
winter of wrong
temperatures. I want to slip on
my mother's raincoat,
invisible skin, fill its pockets
with something that is not
smoke or floodwater.

Downriver

the storm is a girl   on the edge of fury
in a dress the color of lead   not

the girl I once was   *too easy*   let's talk about
downriver parishes no one knows the names of

not a *spill* of moonlight   no cool loose dirt   let's talk
about a river   thrashing   blinking open   no

lovely blur   but a wrecked yellow shotgun
splintered   crushed   yes I am talking about

dynamite   yes *downriver* is a word   take it
apart   I am talking about the levee at Caernarvon

no metaphor   only *spill*   only *break*   only *explode*
not *edge*   yet how often I walked the Mississippi's shore

mud sunk   *swirl of storm*   no   too lovely   tall river grass
levee stunned open   glow of a silvered moon between

split trees   a body swept and dredged

ACKNOWLEDGMENTS

Grateful acknowledgment is made to the editors of the following publications in which the following poems first appeared, sometimes in a slightly different form: *Blackbird:* "Mother Water Ash," "New Orleans Love Poem," and "Sixteen Years to the Day Another Hurricane Reverses"; *Cherry Tree:* "Missing [At the coffee shop]" and "Missing [*Grief is rage*]"; *Court Green:* "Missing [*My mother is a fish*]" and "Missing [Two months after]"; *diode:* "Being the Oldest Daughter"; *Florida Review:* "On the Levee Once Again I Walk to Sharpen"; *Foundry:* "Monochords [*Grief:* necklace burdening]"; *Harbor Review:* "My Mother's Ashtray"; *Ilanot Review:* "Elegy, Napoleon House, New Orleans" and "Still Life, South Galvez Street, 1978"; *Manifest-Station:* "Breathwork"; *PEN America:* "[Another summer of the vanishing. Summer]" and "[Ten years into the After, the Mississippi]"; *Scoundrel Time:* "On the Mississippi River Levee, Styrofoam Cup in My Hand"; *storySouth:* "Still Life, Jefferson Highway"; *SWWIM:* "My Mother's Nightgowns Smell Like Smoke"; *Tupelo Quarterly:* "After My Mother Dies I Crave the Seventies."

"Mourning, Silk and Lace" first appeared in *The Ekphrastic Writer: Creating Art-Influenced Poetry, Fiction and Nonfiction* (McFarland, 2020).

"My Mother's Nightgowns Smell Like Smoke" was also reprinted in the anthology *Braving the Body*, ed. Nicole Callihan, Jennifer Franklin, and Pichchenda Bao (Harbor Editions, an imprint of Small Harbor Publishing, 2024).

~~~~~

I am grateful to the PSC-CUNY Research Award Program from the Research Foundation of the City University of New York for a grant that enabled the writing of this book. I am also grateful for the yearlong sabbatical from CUNY that allowed me to complete it.

Thank you to the New York Public Library in New York City and St. Andrew's Church in New Orleans, both havens.

Enormous gratitude to my students at the City University of New York, both MFA and undergrad, who inspire me to take risks.

I am so grateful to my colleagues from whom I learn so much—Annmarie Drury, Roger Sedarat, Ammiel Alcalay, John Weir, Briallen Hopper, Jason Tougaw.

The staff at LSU Press has been as always a joy to work with on this book—I am supremely lucky to work with James Long, Alisa Plant, Ashley Gilly, Sunny Rosen, James Wilson, and everyone at the press.

Thank you to Ben Zervigon and Alluvium Ensemble for supporting my work.

And thank you to Carolyn Hembree, Tim Liu, John Rice, Brad Richard, for anchoring conversations and friendship.

So much love to: Pamela Barnett, Jodi Cressman, Michelle Frucht, Susan Hinton, Naomi Jackson, Shelley Renee, Siân Silyn Roberts, Carolee Tran, Elizabeth Zervigon.

Amelie Hastie, I am so grateful for your ongoing presence in my life and for your support.

Talia Schaffer, you have taught me immeasurably about care and love.

Nancy Austin, my guide through all of this—thank you.

And to Kimiko Hahn and Julia Spicher Kasdorf, brilliant readers of my poems. I could not write without you and I am so lucky for your careful attention to my work.

And to my sister Alissa, who I treasure always, and my beloved brother, Josh.

Love forever to my father, Peter Cooley; my husband, Alex Hinton; and my daughters, Meridian and Arcadia.

NOTES

"On the Mississippi River Levee, Styrofoam Cup in My Hand": It is estimated that Styrofoam takes up to 500 years to decompose.

"Sixteen Years to the Day Another Hurricane Reverses": On August 29, 2021, the sixteenth anniversary of Hurricane Katrina devastating the Gulf Coast, Hurricane Ida made landfall in Louisiana. This poem is built around that synchronicity.

"Monochords": These poems borrow their titles and forms from Yannis Ritsos.

"[*With each Mississippi River flood, water spills out of the river*]": This poem includes language from the City of New Orleans's Hazard Mitigation Plan for flooding: https://ready.nola.gov/hazard-mitigation/hazards/flooding/.

"[Once the coastline spoke: *I plan to disappear and tell you nothing*]": This poem owes a debt to the book *One Big Self: An Investigation,* written by my first poetry teacher, C. D. Wright.

"Mourning, Silk and Lace": This poem is based on *Embroidered Sampler,* 1799, by Millsent Connor.

"[Could the California Fires ever fill the Mississippi]": According to findings published by *Science Daily* on February 8, 2021, as "Cleaning Up the Mississippi River," "The Mississippi River is the largest river in North America with about 30 million people living within its watershed." Elizabeth Kolbert's *New Yorker* essay "Louisiana's Disappearing Coast," published on March 25, 2019, also inspired me here.

"Downriver": In 1927, the "Great Flood" of the Mississippi River ravaged much of the country. In Louisiana, the river was diverted to flood Black neighborhoods and drive citizens out. Rebecca Solnit and Rebecca Snedeker's *Unfathomable City: A New Orleans Atlas* is an inspiration here. This poem is also sparked by Ada Limón's line "I felt most myself by the river" from her poem "Only the Faintest Blue."

Printed in the USA
CPSIA information can be obtained
at www.ICGtesting.com
CBHW020201100824
12755CB00016B/212

9 780807 182468